LOW POTASSIUM DIET COOKBOOK FOR SENIORS

By

Nora Moyer

Disclaimer

Please bear in mind that the information in this book is strictly educational. The data presented here is claimed to be credible and trustworthy. The author provides no implied or explicit assurance of accuracy for specific individual instances.

It is important that you consult with a skilled practitioner, such as your doctor, before initiating any diet or lifestyle changes. The information in this book should not be used in place of expert advice or professional assistance.

The author, publisher, and distributor fully disclaim any and all liability, loss, damage, or risk suffered by anybody who relies on the information in this book, whether directly or indirectly.

All intellectual property rights are intact. The content in this book should not be copied in any way, mechanically, electronically, by photocopying, or by any other means available.

CONTENTS

Introduction

In the heartwarming opening chapter of this "Low Potassium Diet Cookbook for Seniors," we delve into the inspiring success story of Mary, a fictitious patient whose journey to better health serves as a beacon of hope for all those grappling with the challenges of high potassium levels. Mary's story is one of resilience, determination, and the transformative power of practical dietary choices.

Mary, much like many seniors, faced the daunting reality of health complications associated with high potassium levels. Fatigue, muscle weakness, and a persistent sense of lethargy had become the unwelcome companions of her daily life. Frustrated with the limitations that her health placed on her ability to enjoy life to the fullest, Mary sought out solutions that would empower her to regain control.

Enter the low potassium diet—a simple yet powerful lifestyle change that became Mary's pathway to rejuvenation. Through diligent adherence to a carefully crafted low potassium meal plan, Mary witnessed a remarkable transformation in her overall well-being. The fatigue began to lift, and her energy levels surged. Muscles that once felt weak and unresponsive gained strength, enabling Mary to engage in activities she had long abandoned.

This introductory chapter extends beyond Mary's personal triumph, providing a comprehensive exploration of the importance of a low potassium diet for seniors. We delve into the physiological aspects of potassium regulation within the body and unravel the intricate web of health implications associated with elevated potassium levels in seniors.

High potassium levels, if left unchecked, can lead to serious health issues such as cardiovascular complications and compromised kidney function—conditions particularly prevalent in the senior population. Our aim is to demystify the science behind potassium metabolism and empower readers with the knowledge needed to make informed dietary choices that can contribute to a healthier, more vibrant life.

As we set the stage for the culinary journey that lies ahead, we underscore the pivotal role this cookbook can play in enhancing the quality of life for seniors. Beyond being a mere collection of recipes, this book is a comprehensive guide designed to facilitate a seamless transition to a low potassium lifestyle.

Each chapter is meticulously crafted to address different aspects of a low potassium diet, from understanding the basics and stocking a low potassium kitchen to navigating social situations and dining out with confidence. With an emphasis on practicality, we provide not just recipes but also tips, techniques, and strategies to empower seniors in embracing and sustaining a low potassium lifestyle.

Embark on this culinary adventure with us, and let the pages of this cookbook be your companion in the journey toward improved health, increased energy, and a renewed zest for life. Mary's success story is just the beginning—your own transformative journey awaits within these pages.

Chapter 1: Potassium and Seniors

As we embark on the first chapter of our "Low Potassium Diet Cookbook for Seniors," it's essential to lay the foundation by understanding the intricate relationship between seniors and potassium. This chapter serves as a gateway to unravel the mysteries of potassium's role in the body, shed light on the potential health implications of elevated potassium levels, and explore the myriad benefits that a low potassium diet can offer to seniors seeking to optimize their well-being.

The Role of Potassium in the Body

Potassium, a vital mineral and electrolyte, plays a pivotal role in maintaining the delicate balance required for the proper functioning of our bodies. It is not merely an arbitrary component but an essential contributor to the normal functioning of cells, tissues, and organs. Seniors, like individuals of all age groups, rely on potassium for the regulation of heart rhythm, muscle contractions, and the balance of fluids within and outside cells.

In the intricate dance of bodily functions, potassium acts as a conductor, ensuring that various physiological processes harmonize to sustain life. From the rhythmic beating of the heart to the contraction and relaxation of muscles, potassium is an unsung hero operating behind the scenes, contributing to the seamless orchestration of the body's symphony.

Health Implications of High Potassium Levels in Seniors

However, as with many aspects of health, balance is key. In seniors, the delicate equilibrium of potassium levels can be disrupted, leading to potentially severe health consequences. High potassium levels, known as hyperkalemia, pose specific risks for the aging population. Seniors may be more susceptible to this condition due to factors such as reduced kidney function, medications, and other age-related changes in the body.

Untreated hyperkalemia can manifest in a variety of symptoms, ranging from mild to severe. Fatigue, weakness, irregular heartbeats, and even paralysis are potential outcomes. Understanding these risks is crucial for seniors and their caregivers, as it underscores the importance of proactively managing potassium intake to mitigate potential health issues.

Benefits of a Low Potassium Diet for Seniors

Amidst the challenges posed by high potassium levels, the good news emerges—adopting a low potassium diet can be a game-changer for seniors. This section of the chapter focuses on the positive impact that a thoughtful and well-balanced low potassium diet can have on the health and vitality of seniors.

A carefully curated low potassium diet not only addresses the risks associated with hyperkalemia but also promotes overall well-being. From improved cardiovascular health to enhanced muscle function and reduced fatigue, the benefits are multifaceted. Seniors who embrace a low potassium diet may find themselves experiencing increased energy levels, improved mobility, and a greater sense of control over their health.

As we delve deeper into the subsequent chapters, the knowledge gleaned from this foundational chapter will serve as a compass, guiding seniors toward a healthier and more balanced relationship with potassium, setting the stage for a transformative culinary journey ahead.

Chapter 2: Basics of a Low Potassium Diet

In the second chapter of our "Low Potassium Diet Cookbook for Seniors," we delve into the fundamental building blocks of adopting a low potassium lifestyle. This chapter serves as a practical guide, equipping seniors with the knowledge and skills needed to navigate the complexities of identifying high potassium foods, deciphering food labels for potassium content, and ultimately creating a well-balanced, nutrient-rich diet plan tailored to their unique needs.

Identifying High Potassium Foods

The journey toward a low potassium diet begins with a keen awareness of the foods that are rich in this essential mineral. Seniors will find invaluable information on the potassium content of various food items, ranging from fruits and vegetables to grains, dairy, and protein sources. By understanding which foods are high in potassium, individuals can make informed choices about what to include in their meals and what to moderate or avoid.

This section of the chapter provides a comprehensive list of high potassium foods, empowering seniors to make educated decisions about their dietary intake. Through this knowledge, they gain the ability to construct meals that not only adhere to low potassium guidelines but also cater to their taste preferences and cultural culinary traditions.

Reading Food Labels for Potassium Content

In an era of pre-packaged and convenience foods, deciphering food labels becomes a crucial skill in the quest for a low potassium diet. This section of the chapter acts as a guide to the often-confusing landscape of nutrition labels, offering seniors tips and insights on how to identify and interpret potassium content effectively.

By honing the ability to scrutinize labels, seniors can navigate the grocery store aisles with confidence, selecting foods that align with their dietary goals. Practical examples and case studies illuminate the process, ensuring that the knowledge gained is not just theoretical but readily applicable to real-world scenarios.

Creating a Balanced and Nutrient-Rich Diet Plan

The essence of a successful low potassium diet lies not just in avoiding high-potassium foods but in crafting a well-rounded and nutritionally sound meal plan. This section of the chapter introduces seniors to the art of balancing macronutrients and micronutrients, emphasizing the importance of variety, moderation, and portion control.

Readers will find practical tips on meal prepping, cooking techniques, and culinary substitutions that enhance the flavor and nutritional value of low potassium meals. From breakfast to dinner, this section provides a roadmap for creating meals that are not only compliant with a low potassium diet but also delicious and satisfying.

In this book, seniors will have acquired the foundational knowledge and practical skills necessary to embark on their low potassium journey. Armed with the ability to identify high potassium foods, interpret food labels, and create balanced and nutrient-rich meal plans, they are well-prepared to transform their dietary habits and take a proactive step towards better health and well-being.

Chapter 3: Kitchen Essentials for a Low Potassium Diet

In the culinary exploration of a low potassium lifestyle, Chapter Three of our "Low Potassium Diet Cookbook for Seniors" is dedicated to laying the groundwork within the heart of the home—the kitchen. This chapter serves as a practical guide, unveiling the secrets to stocking a low potassium pantry, introducing essential tools for cooking low potassium meals, and offering invaluable tips for meal preparation and planning. As seniors embark on their journey to embrace a new way of eating, a well-equipped kitchen becomes the cornerstone of success.

Stocking a Low Potassium Pantry

Creating a low potassium pantry is akin to assembling the building blocks for culinary success. This section of the chapter provides a comprehensive list of pantry staples that align with the principles of a low potassium diet. From grains and legumes to herbs, spices, and cooking oils, seniors will discover an array of flavorful and nutrient-rich ingredients that form the basis of diverse and satisfying low potassium meals.

With the pantry as a foundation, seniors can approach meal planning with confidence, knowing that they have a well-stocked arsenal of ingredients that cater to their dietary needs. This section not only presents the what but also the why, elucidating the nutritional benefits of each pantry staple and how they contribute to a balanced and health-conscious diet.

Essential Tools for Cooking Low Potassium Meals

The right tools can transform cooking from a chore into a joy. In this segment, seniors are introduced to a selection of essential kitchen tools that streamline the process of preparing low potassium meals. From versatile knives and cutting boards to specialized gadgets that aid in meal preparation, these tools are chosen with an eye toward efficiency and ease.

Additionally, this section provides tips on how to maximize the utility of each tool, ensuring that seniors can navigate the kitchen with confidence and competence. As they become acquainted with these essential tools, cooking becomes not only a means of sustenance but a pleasurable and empowering activity.

Breakfast Delights

Scrambled Egg Whites with Spinach and Tomatoes

Start your day with a protein-packed and potassium-conscious breakfast. These fluffy scrambled egg whites combined with vibrant spinach and juicy tomatoes create a delicious and nutritious morning meal.

Total Time: 15 minutes
Servings: 2

Ingredients:
- 1 cup egg whites
- 1 cup fresh spinach, chopped
- 1 cup cherry tomatoes, halved
- Salt and pepper to taste
- Cooking spray

Directions:
1. Heat a non-stick skillet over medium heat and coat with cooking spray.
2. Add chopped spinach and cook until wilted.
3. Pour in egg whites, stirring gently until they start to set.
4. Add cherry tomatoes, salt, and pepper. Continue to cook until eggs are fully cooked.
5. Serve hot and enjoy your low potassium, high-protein breakfast!

Nutritional Information: (Per Serving)
- ➢ Calories: 120
- ➢ Protein: 25g
- ➢ Carbohydrates: 5g
- ➢ Fat: 0g

Oatmeal with Fresh Berries and Almond Milk

A comforting and heart-healthy breakfast awaits with this low potassium oatmeal. Topped with a medley of fresh berries and almond milk, it's a wholesome and satisfying way to kickstart your day.

Total Time: 10 minutes
Servings: 2

Ingredients:
- 1 cup rolled oats
- 2 cups almond milk
- 1 cup mixed berries (strawberries, blueberries, raspberries)
- 1 tablespoon honey (optional)
- 1 teaspoon chia seeds (optional)

Directions:
1. Cook rolled oats with almond milk according to package instructions.
2. Once cooked, divide into bowls.
3. Top with mixed berries, drizzle with honey, and sprinkle with chia seeds if desired.
4. Stir and savor a delicious, potassium-conscious breakfast!

Nutritional Information: (Per Serving)
- Calories: 250
- Protein: 8g
- Carbohydrates: 45g
- Fat: 5g

Greek Yogurt Parfait with Low Potassium Fruits

Indulge in the creamy goodness of Greek yogurt paired with a variety of low potassium fruits. This parfait is a delightful and nutrient-rich way to start your morning with a burst of flavor.

Total Time: 5 minutes
Servings: 1

Ingredients:
- 1 cup plain Greek yogurt
- 1/2 cup diced pineapple
- 1/2 cup diced mango
- 1/4 cup sliced strawberries
- 1 tablespoon chopped almonds
- 1 teaspoon honey

Directions:
1. In a glass or bowl, layer Greek yogurt with diced pineapple, mango, and sliced strawberries.
2. Sprinkle chopped almonds on top.
3. Drizzle with honey for a touch of sweetness.
4. Grab a spoon and enjoy this nutritious and satisfying parfait!

Nutritional Information: (Per Serving)
- Calories: 350
- Protein: 20g
- Carbohydrates: 45g
- Fat: 12g

Banana and Blueberry Smoothie Bowl

Dive into a refreshing and potassium-conscious smoothie bowl featuring the dynamic duo of bananas and blueberries. Packed with antioxidants and nutrients, this bowl is a tasty treat for your taste buds and your health.

Total Time: 10 minutes
Servings: 1

Ingredients:
- 1 frozen banana
- 1/2 cup blueberries
- 1/2 cup almond milk
- 1/4 cup granola
- 1 tablespoon chia seeds

- Sliced banana and blueberries for topping

Directions:
1. Blend frozen banana, blueberries, and almond milk until smooth.
2. Pour into a bowl and top with granola, chia seeds, and fresh fruit slices.
3. Grab a spoon and relish the vibrant flavors of this potassium-conscious breakfast!

Nutritional Information: (Per Serving)
- ➢ Calories: 300
- ➢ Protein: 7g
- ➢ Carbohydrates: 60g
- ➢ Fat: 5g

Quinoa Breakfast Bowl with Sliced Strawberries

Elevate your morning routine with a protein-packed quinoa breakfast bowl. Paired with sliced strawberries, this dish offers a delightful blend of textures and flavors while keeping potassium levels in check.

Total Time: 20 minutes
Servings: 2

Ingredients:
- 1 cup cooked quinoa
- 1 cup sliced strawberries
- 1/4 cup chopped walnuts
- 1 tablespoon honey
- 1/2 cup Greek yogurt

Directions:
1. In a bowl, combine cooked quinoa, sliced strawberries, and chopped walnuts.
2. Drizzle honey over the mixture.
3. Top with a dollop of Greek yogurt.
4. Gently stir and savor a nutrient-rich and satisfying quinoa breakfast bowl!

Nutritional Information: (Per Serving)
- ➢ Calories: 280

- ➢ Protein: 8g
- ➢ Carbohydrates: 40g
- ➢ Fat: 10g

Low Potassium Pancakes with Applesauce

Start your morning on a delightful note with these low potassium pancakes. The addition of applesauce not only adds a hint of sweetness but also keeps potassium levels in check, creating a delicious and nutritious breakfast treat.

Total Time: 20 minutes
Servings: 2

Ingredients:
- 1 cup all-purpose flour
- 1 tablespoon sugar
- 1 teaspoon baking powder
- 1/2 teaspoon cinnamon
- 1 cup milk (or non-dairy alternative)
- 1/4 cup unsweetened applesauce
- 1 egg
- Cooking spray for the pan

Directions:
1. In a bowl, whisk together flour, sugar, baking powder, and cinnamon.
2. In a separate bowl, combine milk, applesauce, and egg.
3. Add the wet ingredients to the dry ingredients, stirring until just combined.
4. Heat a griddle or pan over medium heat and coat with cooking spray.
5. Pour 1/4 cup of batter onto the griddle for each pancake.
6. Cook until bubbles form on the surface, then flip and cook the other side.
7. Serve hot with your favorite toppings and enjoy these low potassium pancakes!

Nutritional Information: (Per Serving)
- ➢ Calories: 250
- ➢ Protein: 8g
- ➢ Carbohydrates: 45g
- ➢ Fat: 4g

Cottage Cheese and Peach Stuffed Crepes

Elevate your breakfast experience with these luscious stuffed crepes. The combination of creamy cottage cheese and sweet peaches creates a delightful contrast of textures, making this dish a morning favorite.

Total Time: 30 minutes
Servings: 2

Ingredients:
- 1 cup all-purpose flour
- 1 1/2 cups milk
- 2 eggs
- 1 tablespoon melted butter
- 1 cup cottage cheese
- 1 cup diced peaches (fresh or canned, drained)
- Honey for drizzling (optional)

Directions:
1. In a blender, combine flour, milk, eggs, and melted butter. Blend until smooth.
2. Heat a non-stick skillet over medium heat and pour in a small amount of batter, swirling to coat the pan evenly.
3. Cook each crepe for 1-2 minutes on each side until lightly golden.
4. In a bowl, mix cottage cheese and diced peaches.
5. Spoon the cottage cheese and peach mixture into the center of each crepe, then fold.
6. Drizzle with honey if desired and serve warm.

Nutritional Information: (Per Serving)
- ➢ Calories: 380
- ➢ Protein: 20g
- ➢ Carbohydrates: 50g
- ➢ Fat: 12g

Avocado Toast with Lemon and Chia Seeds

Experience a trendy and nutrient-packed breakfast with this avocado toast. The creamy avocado, zesty lemon, and chia seeds create a powerhouse of flavors and health benefits, making it a perfect start to your day.

Total Time: 10 minutes
Servings: 1

Ingredients:
- 1 slice whole-grain bread
- 1/2 ripe avocado, mashed
- 1 teaspoon chia seeds
- Lemon zest (from half a lemon)
- Salt and pepper to taste

Directions:
1. Toast the whole-grain bread to your liking.
2. Spread the mashed avocado over the toasted bread.
3. Sprinkle chia seeds evenly on top.
4. Grate lemon zest over the avocado.
5. Season with salt and pepper to taste.
6. Enjoy this simple, yet flavorful, low potassium breakfast!

Nutritional Information: (Per Serving)
- Calories: 230
- Protein: 5g
- Carbohydrates: 20g
- Fat: 15g

Sweet Potato Hash with Poached Eggs

Dive into a savory and satisfying breakfast with this sweet potato hash. Paired with perfectly poached eggs, this dish offers a balance of textures and flavors, creating a nutritious and filling morning meal.

Total Time: 25 minutes
Servings: 2
Ingredients:
- 2 medium sweet potatoes, peeled and grated
- 1 tablespoon olive oil
- 1/2 onion, diced
- 1 bell pepper, diced
- 2 cloves garlic, minced
- 4 large eggs
- Salt and pepper to taste
- Fresh parsley for garnish (optional)

Directions:
1. In a large skillet, heat olive oil over medium heat.
2. Add grated sweet potatoes, onion, bell pepper, and garlic. Cook until sweet potatoes are tender and slightly crispy.
3. Create four wells in the hash and crack an egg into each well.
4. Cover the skillet and cook until the eggs are poached to your liking.
5. Season with salt and pepper, garnish with fresh parsley if desired, and serve hot.

Nutritional Information: (Per Serving)
➢ Calories: 320
➢ Protein: 14g
➢ Carbohydrates: 40g
➢ Fat: 12g

Whole Grain Waffles with Raspberry Sauce

Enjoy a wholesome and fruity breakfast with these whole grain waffles topped with a luscious raspberry sauce. The combination of whole grains and fresh fruit creates a delightful and nutritious morning treat.

Total Time: 15 minutes

Servings: 2

Ingredients:
- 1 cup whole wheat flour
- 1 tablespoon sugar
- 1 teaspoon baking powder
- 1/2 teaspoon cinnamon
- 1 cup milk (or non-dairy alternative)
- 1 egg
- Cooking spray for the waffle iron
- 1 cup fresh raspberries
- 2 tablespoons maple syrup

Directions:
1. In a bowl, whisk together whole wheat flour, sugar, baking powder, and cinnamon.
2. In a separate bowl, combine milk and egg.
3. Add the wet ingredients to the dry ingredients, stirring until just combined.
4. Preheat the waffle iron and coat with cooking spray.
5. Pour batter onto the waffle iron and cook according to manufacturer instructions.
6. In a small saucepan, heat raspberries and maple syrup until the berries break down and the mixture thickens.
7. Serve waffles topped with warm raspberry sauce.

Nutritional Information: (Per Serving)
- Calories: 300
- Protein: 10g
- Carbohydrates: 60g
- Fat: 5g

Chia Seed Pudding with Mango

Delight your taste buds with this wholesome chia seed pudding topped with sweet, ripe mango. Packed with fiber, omega-3 fatty acids, and a burst of tropical flavor, this breakfast is as nutritious as it is delicious.

Total Time: 4 hours (including chilling time)

Servings: 2

Ingredients:
- 1/4 cup chia seeds
- 1 cup almond milk
- 1 tablespoon honey
- 1/2 teaspoon vanilla extract
- 1 ripe mango, diced

Directions:
1. In a bowl, mix chia seeds, almond milk, honey, and vanilla extract.
2. Cover and refrigerate for at least 4 hours or overnight until the mixture thickens.
3. Stir well before serving.
4. Spoon chia pudding into bowls and top with diced mango.
5. Enjoy a delightful and nutrient-packed start to your day!

Nutritional Information: (Per Serving)
- Calories: 220
- Protein: 5g
- Carbohydrates: 30g
- Fat: 10g

Veggie and Egg White Breakfast Burrito

Fuel your morning with this protein-packed, low potassium breakfast burrito. Loaded with egg whites and an assortment of colorful vegetables, this burrito is a satisfying and nutritious way to kickstart your day.

Total Time: 15 minutes
Servings: 1

Ingredients:
- 2 large egg whites
- 1 whole wheat tortilla
- 1/4 cup diced bell peppers (any color)
- 1/4 cup diced tomatoes
- 2 tablespoons diced red onion
- 1/4 cup spinach, chopped
- Salt and pepper to taste

- Salsa for topping (optional)

Directions:
1. In a skillet, cook egg whites until fully set.
2. Warm the whole wheat tortilla in the skillet or microwave.
3. Layer cooked egg whites, diced bell peppers, tomatoes, red onion, and chopped spinach on the tortilla.
4. Season with salt and pepper.
5. Roll into a burrito and, if desired, top with salsa.
6. Indulge in a hearty and nutrient-rich breakfast burrito!

Nutritional Information: (Per Serving)
- ➤ Calories: 280
- ➤ Protein: 20g
- ➤ Carbohydrates: 40g
- ➤ Fat: 5g

Cranberry Walnut Muffins

Start your day on a sweet note with these delectable cranberry walnut muffins. Bursting with fruity goodness and the crunch of walnuts, these muffins are a delightful addition to your low potassium breakfast repertoire.

Total Time: 30 minutes
Servings: 12

Ingredients:
- 2 cups all-purpose flour
- 1/2 cup sugar
- 1 tablespoon baking powder
- 1/2 teaspoon salt
- 1 cup almond milk
- 1/4 cup vegetable oil
- 1 teaspoon vanilla extract
- 1 cup fresh or frozen cranberries
- 1/2 cup chopped walnuts

Directions:
1. Preheat the oven to 375°F (190°C) and line a muffin tin with paper liners.
2. In a bowl, whisk together flour, sugar, baking powder, and salt.

3. In a separate bowl, mix almond milk, vegetable oil, and vanilla extract.
4. Combine wet and dry ingredients, stirring until just combined.
5. Fold in cranberries and chopped walnuts.
6. Divide batter evenly among muffin cups and bake for 20-25 minutes or until a toothpick comes out clean.
7. Allow to cool before enjoying these flavorful muffins!

Nutritional Information: (Per Serving)
➢ Calories: 180
➢ Protein: 3g
➢ Carbohydrates: 25g
➢ Fat: 8g

Almond Flour Banana Bread

Savor the comforting aroma of freshly baked banana bread without compromising your low potassium diet. This almond flour banana bread is moist, flavorful, and a guilt-free delight for your breakfast table.

Total Time: 1 hour
Servings: 8

Ingredients:
• 2 cups almond flour
• 1 teaspoon baking powder
• 1/2 teaspoon baking soda
• 1/4 teaspoon salt
• 3 ripe bananas, mashed
• 1/4 cup honey
• 1/4 cup coconut oil, melted
• 2 large eggs
• 1 teaspoon vanilla extract
• 1/2 cup chopped almonds for topping (optional)

Directions:
1. Preheat the oven to 350°F (175°C) and grease a loaf pan.
2. In a bowl, whisk together almond flour, baking powder, baking soda, and salt.
3. In a separate bowl, mix mashed bananas, honey, melted coconut oil, eggs, and vanilla extract.
4. Combine wet and dry ingredients, stirring until well combined.

5. Pour the batter into the prepared loaf pan.
6. If desired, sprinkle chopped almonds on top.
7. Bake for 45-50 minutes or until a toothpick comes out clean.
8. Let it cool before slicing and enjoying this low potassium banana bread!

Nutritional Information: (Per Serving)
➢ Calories: 250
➢ Protein: 7g
➢ Carbohydrates: 20g
➢ Fat: 16g

Breakfast Frittata with Low Potassium Vegetables

Elevate your breakfast with a colorful and nutritious frittata featuring low potassium vegetables. This easy-to-make dish is versatile, allowing you to incorporate your favorite veggies for a delightful morning meal.

Total Time: 25 minutes
Servings: 4

Ingredients:
- 8 large egg whites
- 1 cup diced zucchini
- 1/2 cup diced bell peppers (any color)
- 1/2 cup cherry tomatoes, halved
- 1/4 cup diced red onion
- 1/4 cup chopped fresh parsley
- Salt and pepper to taste
- Cooking spray

Directions:
1. Preheat the oven to 350°F (175°C).
2. In a bowl, whisk together egg whites, salt, and pepper.
3. Heat an oven-safe skillet over medium heat and coat with cooking spray.
4. Add diced zucchini, bell peppers, cherry tomatoes, and red onion to the skillet. Cook until vegetables are slightly softened.
5. Pour the whisked egg whites over the vegetables, ensuring an even distribution.

6. Sprinkle chopped parsley on top.
7. Transfer the skillet to the preheated oven and bake for 15-20 minutes or until the frittata is set.
8. Slice and serve this delightful and low potassium breakfast frittata!

Nutritional Information: (Per Serving)
- ➤ Calories: 100
- ➤ Protein: 15g
- ➤ Carbohydrates: 5g
- ➤ Fat: 2g

Lunchtime Favorites

Grilled Chicken Salad with Mixed Greens and Balsamic Vinaigrette

Energize your afternoon with a Grilled Chicken Salad featuring a medley of mixed greens and a tangy balsamic vinaigrette. This vibrant and nutrient-rich salad is a perfect balance of flavors and textures.

Total Time: 20 minutes
Servings: 2

Ingredients:
- 2 boneless, skinless chicken breasts
- 6 cups mixed salad greens
- 1 cup cherry tomatoes, halved
- 1/2 cucumber, sliced
- 1/4 cup red onion, thinly sliced
- 1/4 cup feta cheese, crumbled
- 2 tablespoons balsamic vinaigrette dressing

Directions:
1. Season chicken breasts with salt and pepper and grill until fully cooked.
2. Slice grilled chicken into strips.
3. In a large bowl, combine mixed greens, cherry tomatoes, cucumber, red onion, and grilled chicken.
4. Drizzle with balsamic vinaigrette dressing and toss gently.
5. Sprinkle feta cheese on top and serve this refreshing and nutritious grilled chicken salad!

Nutritional Information: (Per Serving)
- Calories: 350
- Protein: 30g
- Carbohydrates: 15g
- Fat: 18g

Lentil Soup with Carrots and Kale

Embrace a warm and comforting lunch with this hearty Lentil Soup featuring carrots and kale. Packed with fiber and protein, this soup is a wholesome and satisfying option for a low potassium diet.

Total Time: 40 minutes
Servings: 4

Ingredients:
- 1 cup dried green lentils, rinsed and drained
- 1 tablespoon olive oil
- 1 onion, diced
- 2 carrots, diced
- 2 cloves garlic, minced
- 1 teaspoon cumin
- 1 teaspoon smoked paprika
- 6 cups vegetable broth
- 2 cups chopped kale
- Salt and pepper to taste
- Lemon wedges for serving

Directions:
1. In a large pot, heat olive oil over medium heat.
2. Add diced onion, carrots, and garlic. Sauté until softened.
3. Stir in cumin and smoked paprika.
4. Add lentils and vegetable broth, bringing to a boil.
5. Reduce heat, cover, and simmer for 25-30 minutes or until lentils are tender.
6. Stir in chopped kale and cook until wilted.
7. Season with salt and pepper.
8. Serve hot with a squeeze of lemon and enjoy this nutritious lentil soup!

Nutritional Information: (Per Serving)
- Calories: 250
- Protein: 15g
- Carbohydrates: 40g
- Fat: 5g

Turkey and Avocado Wrap with Whole Wheat Tortilla

Experience a light and satisfying lunch with a Turkey and Avocado Wrap featuring a whole wheat tortilla. Packed with lean turkey, creamy avocado, and crisp vegetables, this wrap is a delicious and portable option.

Total Time: 15 minutes
Servings: 2

Ingredients:
- 4 whole wheat tortillas
- 1/2 pound sliced turkey breast
- 1 avocado, sliced
- 1 cup mixed greens
- 1/2 cup cherry tomatoes, halved
- 2 tablespoons Greek yogurt (optional)
- Salt and pepper to taste

Directions:
1. Lay out the whole wheat tortillas on a flat surface.
2. Divide the sliced turkey, avocado, mixed greens, and cherry tomatoes among the tortillas.
3. Optional: Drizzle with Greek yogurt for added creaminess.
4. Season with salt and pepper.
5. Fold the sides of the tortilla and roll up into a wrap.
6. Slice in half and enjoy this simple and nutritious turkey and avocado wrap!

Nutritional Information: (Per Serving)
- Calories: 350
- Protein: 25g
- Carbohydrates: 30g
- Fat: 15g

Quinoa Salad with Cucumber, Tomato, and Feta

Elevate your lunch with a refreshing Quinoa Salad featuring crisp cucumbers, juicy tomatoes, and tangy feta cheese. This protein-packed salad is a delightful and satisfying option for a low potassium meal.

Total Time: 25 minutes
Servings: 4

Ingredients:
- 1 cup quinoa, rinsed and cooked
- 1 cucumber, diced
- 1 cup cherry tomatoes, halved
- 1/4 cup red onion, finely chopped
- 1/2 cup feta cheese, crumbled
- 1/4 cup fresh parsley, chopped
- 2 tablespoons olive oil
- 2 tablespoons balsamic vinegar
- Salt and pepper to taste

Directions:
1. In a large bowl, combine cooked quinoa, diced cucumber, cherry tomatoes, red onion, feta cheese, and fresh parsley.
2. In a small bowl, whisk together olive oil and balsamic vinegar.
3. Drizzle the dressing over the salad and toss to combine.
4. Season with salt and pepper to taste.
5. Serve chilled and enjoy this vibrant and nutrient-rich quinoa salad!

Nutritional Information: (Per Serving)
- Calories: 280
- Protein: 8g
- Carbohydrates: 35g
- Fat: 12g

Salmon and Asparagus Stir-Fry

Dive into a flavorful and nutritious lunch with this Salmon and Asparagus Stir-Fry. Packed with omega-3 fatty acids and a medley of colorful vegetables, this stir-fry is a quick and delicious option for a low potassium meal.

Total Time: 20 minutes
Servings: 2

Ingredients:
- 2 salmon fillets, skinless
- 1 bunch asparagus, trimmed and cut into 2-inch pieces
- 1 red bell pepper, thinly sliced
- 2 cloves garlic, minced
- 1 tablespoon ginger, grated
- 2 tablespoons low-sodium soy sauce
- 1 tablespoon sesame oil
- 1 teaspoon honey
- Cooked brown rice for serving

Directions:
1. Season salmon fillets with salt and pepper.
2. In a large skillet, heat sesame oil over medium-high heat.
3. Add salmon fillets and cook for 3-4 minutes on each side or until fully cooked. Remove from the skillet and set aside.
4. In the same skillet, add asparagus, red bell pepper, garlic, and ginger. Stir-fry for 5-6 minutes until vegetables are tender-crisp.
5. In a small bowl, whisk together soy sauce and honey. Pour over the vegetable mixture.
6. Flake the cooked salmon and add it to the skillet, gently tossing to combine.
7. Serve over cooked brown rice and enjoy this savory and low potassium salmon and asparagus stir-fry!

Nutritional Information: (Per Serving)
- Calories: 400
- Protein: 30g
- Carbohydrates: 30g
- Fat: 20g

Chickpea and Vegetable Stir-Fry

Elevate your lunch with this Chickpea and Vegetable Stir-Fry, a colorful and protein-packed dish. The combination of chickpeas, vibrant vegetables, and flavorful stir-fry sauce creates a satisfying and nutritious meal.

Total Time: 20 minutes
Servings: 4

Ingredients:
- 2 cans chickpeas, drained and rinsed
- 2 cups broccoli florets
- 1 red bell pepper, sliced
- 1 yellow bell pepper, sliced
- 1 carrot, julienned
- 2 tablespoons soy sauce
- 1 tablespoon sesame oil
- 1 tablespoon rice vinegar
- 1 tablespoon honey
- 1 teaspoon ginger, minced
- 2 cloves garlic, minced
- Cooked brown rice for serving

Directions:
1. In a wok or large skillet, heat sesame oil over medium-high heat.
2. Add chickpeas, broccoli, red and yellow bell peppers, and julienned carrot. Stir-fry for 5-7 minutes until vegetables are tender-crisp.
3. In a small bowl, whisk together soy sauce, rice vinegar, honey, ginger, and garlic.
4. Pour the sauce over the stir-fry and toss to coat.
5. Serve the chickpea and vegetable stir-fry over cooked brown rice and enjoy this quick and nutritious lunch!

Nutritional Information: (Per Serving)
- Calories: 300
- Protein: 12g
- Carbohydrates: 45g
- Fat: 8g

Spinach and Strawberry Salad with Goat Cheese

Indulge in a refreshing Spinach and Strawberry Salad with Goat Cheese, a delightful combination of sweet and savory flavors. This vibrant salad is not only delicious but also packed with vitamins and antioxidants.

Total Time: 15 minutes
Servings: 2

Ingredients:
- 4 cups fresh spinach leaves
- 1 cup strawberries, sliced
- 1/2 cup crumbled goat cheese
- 1/4 cup chopped walnuts
- Balsamic vinaigrette dressing

Directions:
1. In a large bowl, combine fresh spinach, sliced strawberries, crumbled goat cheese, and chopped walnuts.
2. Drizzle with balsamic vinaigrette dressing and toss gently.
3. Serve this Spinach and Strawberry Salad as a light and flavorful lunch option!

Nutritional Information: (Per Serving)
- Calories: 250
- Protein: 8g
- Carbohydrates: 20g
- Fat: 16g

Tuna Salad Lettuce Wraps

Enjoy a light and protein-packed lunch with these Tuna Salad Lettuce Wraps. The combination of tuna, crunchy vegetables, and a zesty dressing creates a satisfying and low-carb meal.

Total Time: 15 minutes
Servings: 2

Ingredients:
- 2 cans tuna, drained
- 1/4 cup mayonnaise
- 1 tablespoon Dijon mustard
- 1 celery stalk, finely chopped
- 1/4 cup red onion, finely chopped
- Salt and pepper to taste
- Butter lettuce leaves for wrapping

Directions:
1. In a bowl, mix tuna, mayonnaise, Dijon mustard, chopped celery, and red onion.
2. Season with salt and pepper to taste.
3. Spoon tuna salad into butter lettuce leaves to create wraps.
4. Serve these Tuna Salad Lettuce Wraps for a light and protein-rich lunch!

Nutritional Information: (Per Serving)
- Calories: 280
- Protein: 20g
- Carbohydrates: 5g
- Fat: 20g

Roasted Vegetable and Brown Rice Bowl

Embrace a wholesome and filling lunch with this Roasted Vegetable and Brown Rice Bowl. The combination of roasted vegetables, hearty brown rice, and a drizzle of tahini creates a satisfying and nutritious meal.

Total Time: 30 minutes
Servings: 4

Ingredients:
- 2 cups broccoli florets
- 2 bell peppers, diced
- 1 zucchini, sliced
- 1 red onion, sliced
- 2 tablespoons olive oil
- 1 teaspoon cumin
- 1 teaspoon paprika
- Salt and pepper to taste

- 2 cups cooked brown rice
- Tahini for drizzling

Directions:
1. Preheat the oven to 400°F (200°C).
2. In a large baking sheet, toss broccoli, bell peppers, zucchini, and red onion with olive oil, cumin, paprika, salt, and pepper.
3. Roast in the oven for 20-25 minutes or until vegetables are tender and slightly caramelized.
4. Divide cooked brown rice among bowls and top with roasted vegetables.
5. Drizzle with tahini and enjoy this Roasted Vegetable and Brown Rice Bowl!

Nutritional Information: (Per Serving)
➢ Calories: 350
➢ Protein: 8g
➢ Carbohydrates: 60g
➢ Fat: 10g

Shrimp and Broccoli Quinoa Bowl

Dive into a protein-packed and nutritious lunch with this Shrimp and Broccoli Quinoa Bowl. The combination of succulent shrimp, crisp broccoli, and fluffy quinoa creates a delicious and balanced meal.

Total Time: 25 minutes
Servings: 2

Ingredients:
- 1 cup quinoa, rinsed and cooked
- 1/2 pound shrimp, peeled and deveined
- 2 cups broccoli florets
- 2 tablespoons olive oil
- 2 cloves garlic, minced
- 1 teaspoon red pepper flakes (optional)
- Salt and pepper to taste
- Lemon wedges for serving

Directions:

1. In a skillet, heat olive oil over medium-high heat.
2. Add shrimp, garlic, and red pepper flakes (if using). Cook until shrimp are pink and opaque.
3. Add broccoli to the skillet and sauté until tender-crisp.
4. Season with salt and pepper to taste.
5. Divide cooked quinoa among bowls and top with shrimp and broccoli.
6. Serve with lemon wedges and enjoy this Shrimp and Broccoli Quinoa Bowl!

Nutritional Information: (Per Serving)
➢ Calories: 400
➢ Protein: 25g
➢ Carbohydrates: 40g
➢ Fat: 15g

Caprese Salad with Balsamic Glaze

Delight your senses with a classic Caprese Salad featuring fresh tomatoes, mozzarella, and basil drizzled with a tangy balsamic glaze. This vibrant and flavorful salad is a perfect light lunch option.

Total Time: 10 minutes
Servings: 2

Ingredients:
- 2 large tomatoes, sliced
- 1 ball fresh mozzarella, sliced
- Fresh basil leaves
- Balsamic glaze
- Salt and pepper to taste

Directions:
1. Arrange alternating slices of tomatoes and mozzarella on a serving platter.
2. Tuck fresh basil leaves between the slices.
3. Drizzle with balsamic glaze.
4. Season with salt and pepper to taste.
5. Enjoy this refreshing Caprese Salad as a quick and elegant lunch!

Nutritional Information: (Per Serving)
➢ Calories: 200

- ➢ Protein: 12g
- ➢ Carbohydrates: 8g
- ➢ Fat: 15g

Zucchini Noodles with Pesto and Cherry Tomatoes

Dive into a bowl of Zucchini Noodles with Pesto and Cherry Tomatoes, a low-carb and flavorful lunch option. This dish combines the freshness of zucchini with the richness of pesto for a satisfying meal.

Total Time: 15 minutes
Servings: 2

Ingredients:
- 4 medium zucchinis, spiralized into noodles
- 1/2 cup basil pesto
- 1 cup cherry tomatoes, halved
- Parmesan cheese for garnish (optional)
- Pine nuts for garnish (optional)

Directions:
1. Spiralize zucchinis into noodles.
2. In a pan, sauté zucchini noodles over medium heat until just tender.
3. Toss the zucchini noodles with basil pesto.
4. Add cherry tomatoes and stir until warmed.
5. Garnish with Parmesan cheese and pine nuts if desired.
6. Serve this Zucchini Noodles with Pesto and Cherry Tomatoes for a light and satisfying lunch!

Nutritional Information: (Per Serving)
- ➢ Calories: 300
- ➢ Protein: 8g
- ➢ Carbohydrates: 15g
- ➢ Fat: 25g

Low Sodium Minestrone Soup

Warm up with a comforting bowl of Low Sodium Minestrone Soup, filled with hearty vegetables and flavorful broth. This soup is a nourishing and satisfying option for a wholesome lunch.

Total Time: 30 minutes
Servings: 4

Ingredients:
- 1 tablespoon olive oil
- 1 onion, diced
- 2 carrots, sliced
- 2 celery stalks, diced
- 2 cloves garlic, minced
- 1 can (14 oz) diced tomatoes
- 1 can (15 oz) low sodium kidney beans, drained and rinsed
- 4 cups low sodium vegetable broth
- 1 cup green beans, chopped
- 1 cup small pasta
- 1 teaspoon Italian seasoning
- Salt and pepper to taste
- Fresh basil for garnish (optional)

Directions:
1. In a large pot, heat olive oil over medium heat.
2. Add diced onion, sliced carrots, diced celery, and minced garlic. Sauté until vegetables are softened.
3. Add diced tomatoes, kidney beans, vegetable broth, green beans, pasta, Italian seasoning, salt, and pepper.
4. Bring to a boil, then reduce heat and simmer for 15-20 minutes or until pasta is cooked.
5. Garnish with fresh basil if desired.

6. Serve this Low Sodium Minestrone Soup for a comforting and heart-healthy lunch!

Nutritional Information: (Per Serving)
- ➢ Calories: 250
- ➢ Protein: 10g
- ➢ Carbohydrates: 45g
- ➢ Fat: 5g

Egg Salad Stuffed Bell Peppers

Enjoy a unique twist on the classic egg salad with these Egg Salad Stuffed Bell Peppers. This low-carb lunch option combines creamy egg salad with the crispness of bell peppers for a satisfying and nutritious meal.

Total Time: 15 minutes
Servings: 2

Ingredients:
- 4 hard-boiled eggs, chopped
- 1/4 cup mayonnaise
- 1 teaspoon Dijon mustard
- 2 green bell peppers, halved and seeds removed
- Salt and pepper to taste
- Paprika for garnish (optional)
- Chopped chives for garnish (optional)

Directions:
1. In a bowl, mix chopped hard-boiled eggs, mayonnaise, and Dijon mustard.
2. Season with salt and pepper to taste.
3. Spoon the egg salad into halved bell peppers.
4. Garnish with paprika and chopped chives if desired.
5. Serve these Egg Salad Stuffed Bell Peppers for a refreshing and low-carb lunch!

Nutritional Information: (Per Serving)
- ➢ Calories: 280
- ➢ Protein: 12g
- ➢ Carbohydrates: 10g

➢ Fat: 20g

Chicken and Vegetable Kebabs

Fire up the grill for these flavorful Chicken and Vegetable Kebabs. This lunch option combines marinated chicken with colorful vegetables, creating a delicious and protein-rich meal.

Total Time: 30 minutes (including marination time)
Servings: 4

Ingredients:
- 1 pound boneless, skinless chicken breast, cut into chunks
- 1 zucchini, sliced
- 1 bell pepper (any color), diced
- 1 red onion, diced
- Cherry tomatoes
- Olive oil
- Lemon juice
- Garlic powder
- Paprika
- Salt and pepper to taste
- Wooden skewers, soaked in water

Directions:
1. In a bowl, mix olive oil, lemon juice, garlic powder, paprika, salt, and pepper to create a marinade.
2. Thread marinated chicken, zucchini, bell pepper, red onion, and cherry tomatoes onto skewers.
3. Preheat the grill to medium-high heat.
4. Grill kebabs for 10-15 minutes, turning occasionally, until chicken is cooked through and vegetables are charred.

5. Serve these Chicken and Vegetable Kebabs for a flavorful and protein-packed lunch!

Nutritional Information: (Per Serving)
- ➢ Calories: 300
- ➢ Protein: 25g
- ➢ Carbohydrates: 10g
- ➢ Fat: 15g

Dinner Delicacies

Baked Lemon Herb Chicken Breast

Elevate your dinner with Baked Lemon Herb Chicken Breast, a flavorful and juicy dish that's easy to prepare. The combination of zesty lemon and aromatic herbs creates a delightful and healthy main course.

Total Time: 30 minutes
Servings: 4

Ingredients:
- 4 boneless, skinless chicken breasts
- 2 tablespoons olive oil
- Zest and juice of 1 lemon
- 2 cloves garlic, minced
- 1 teaspoon dried thyme
- 1 teaspoon dried rosemary
- Salt and pepper to taste
- Fresh parsley for garnish (optional)

Directions:
1. Preheat the oven to 400°F (200°C).
2. In a bowl, mix olive oil, lemon zest, lemon juice, minced garlic, dried thyme, dried rosemary, salt, and pepper.
3. Place chicken breasts in a baking dish and coat with the lemon herb mixture.

4. Bake for 20-25 minutes or until the chicken reaches an internal temperature of 165°F (74°C).
5. Garnish with fresh parsley if desired.
6. Serve this Baked Lemon Herb Chicken Breast for a delicious and aromatic dinner!

Nutritional Information: (Per Serving)
- ➤ Calories: 250
- ➤ Protein: 30g
- ➤ Carbohydrates: 1g
- ➤ Fat: 14g

Baked Cod with Lemon and Dill

Enjoy a light and flavorful dinner with Baked Cod featuring the bright notes of lemon and dill. This dish is quick to prepare, allowing the natural flavors of the cod to shine.

Total Time: 20 minutes
Servings: 4

Ingredients:
- 4 cod fillets
- 2 tablespoons olive oil
- Zest and juice of 1 lemon
- 2 tablespoons fresh dill, chopped
- Salt and pepper to taste
- Lemon slices for garnish (optional)

Directions:
1. Preheat the oven to 400°F (200°C).
2. Place cod fillets in a baking dish.
3. In a bowl, mix olive oil, lemon zest, lemon juice, chopped dill, salt, and pepper.
4. Pour the mixture over the cod fillets, ensuring they are well coated.
5. Bake for 12-15 minutes or until the cod is opaque and flakes easily.
6. Garnish with lemon slices if desired.
7. Serve this Baked Cod with Lemon and Dill for a light and flavorful dinner!

Nutritional Information: (Per Serving)

- ➤ Calories: 180
- ➤ Protein: 25g
- ➤ Carbohydrates: 1g
- ➤ Fat: 8g

Grilled Portobello Mushrooms with Quinoa

Treat yourself to a satisfying and meaty vegetarian dinner with Grilled Portobello Mushrooms served over a bed of fluffy quinoa. This dish is not only delicious but also packed with protein and nutrients.

Total Time: 30 minutes
Servings: 2

Ingredients:
- 4 large Portobello mushrooms, cleaned and stems removed
- 2 tablespoons balsamic vinegar
- 2 tablespoons olive oil
- 2 cloves garlic, minced
- 1 teaspoon dried oregano
- Salt and pepper to taste
- 1 cup quinoa, rinsed and cooked
- Fresh parsley for garnish (optional)

Directions:
1. Preheat the grill or grill pan over medium-high heat.
2. In a bowl, whisk together balsamic vinegar, olive oil, minced garlic, dried oregano, salt, and pepper.
3. Brush the Portobello mushrooms with the marinade.
4. Grill the mushrooms for 4-5 minutes on each side.
5. Serve the grilled Portobello mushrooms over a bed of cooked quinoa.

6. Garnish with fresh parsley if desired.
7. Enjoy these Grilled Portobello Mushrooms with Quinoa for a hearty and nutritious dinner!

Nutritional Information: (Per Serving)
➢ Calories: 300
➢ Protein: 10g
➢ Carbohydrates: 45g
➢ Fat: 10g

Turkey and Vegetable Stuffed Bell Peppers

Indulge in a wholesome and colorful dinner with Turkey and Vegetable Stuffed Bell Peppers. Packed with lean ground turkey and a medley of vegetables, this dish is a well-balanced and satisfying meal.

Total Time: 45 minutes
Servings: 4

Ingredients:
- 4 large bell peppers, halved and seeds removed
- 1 pound lean ground turkey
- 1 cup cooked quinoa
- 1 cup black beans, drained and rinsed
- 1 cup corn kernels
- 1 cup diced tomatoes
- 1 teaspoon cumin
- 1 teaspoon chili powder
- Salt and pepper to taste
- 1 cup shredded cheddar cheese
- Fresh cilantro for garnish (optional)

Directions:
1. Preheat the oven to 375°F (190°C).
2. In a skillet, cook ground turkey until browned.

3. In a large bowl, mix cooked turkey, cooked quinoa, black beans, corn, diced tomatoes, cumin, chili powder, salt, and pepper.
4. Stuff each bell pepper half with the turkey and vegetable mixture.
5. Top with shredded cheddar cheese.
6. Bake for 25-30 minutes or until peppers are tender.
7. Garnish with fresh cilantro if desired.
8. Serve these Turkey and Vegetable Stuffed Bell Peppers for a flavorful and nutritious dinner!

Nutritional Information: (Per Serving)
➤ Calories: 350
➤ Protein: 30g
➤ Carbohydrates: 30g
➤ Fat: 15g

Spaghetti Squash with Tomato Basil Sauce

Embrace a low-carb and vegetable-rich dinner with Spaghetti Squash topped with a flavorful Tomato Basil Sauce. This dish offers a satisfying alternative to traditional pasta while providing a burst of fresh and aromatic flavors.

Total Time: 40 minutes
Servings: 2

Ingredients:
• 1 medium spaghetti squash, halved and seeds removed
• 2 tablespoons olive oil
• 2 cloves garlic, minced
• 1 can (14 oz) crushed tomatoes
• 1/4 cup fresh basil, chopped
• Salt and pepper to taste
• Grated Parmesan cheese for garnish (optional)

Directions:
1. Preheat the oven to 400°F (200°C).
2. Drizzle the cut sides of the spaghetti squash with olive oil and season with salt and pepper.

3. Place the squash halves, cut side down, on a baking sheet and roast for 30-35 minutes or until tender.
4. In a saucepan, sauté minced garlic in olive oil until fragrant.
5. Add crushed tomatoes and chopped fresh basil. Simmer for 10 minutes.
6. Scrape the cooked spaghetti squash with a fork to create "noodles."
7. Serve the spaghetti squash with the tomato basil sauce.
8. Garnish with grated Parmesan cheese if desired.
9. Enjoy this Spaghetti Squash with Tomato Basil Sauce as a delicious and healthy dinner!

Nutritional Information: (Per Serving)
➢ Calories: 250
➢ Protein: 4g
➢ Carbohydrates: 30g
➢ Fat: 14g

Stir-Fried Tofu with Broccoli and Brown Rice

Dive into a plant-based dinner with Stir-Fried Tofu featuring vibrant broccoli and wholesome brown rice. This dish combines the richness of tofu with the crunch of broccoli, creating a satisfying and nutritious meal.

Total Time: 25 minutes
Servings: 4

Ingredients:
- 1 block firm tofu, pressed and cubed
- 2 cups broccoli florets
- 2 tablespoons soy sauce
- 1 tablespoon sesame oil
- 1 tablespoon maple syrup or agave nectar
- 2 tablespoons vegetable oil
- 2 cloves garlic, minced
- 1 teaspoon ginger, grated
- 2 cups cooked brown rice

Directions:

1. In a bowl, mix soy sauce, sesame oil, and maple syrup.
2. Heat vegetable oil in a wok or large skillet over medium-high heat.
3. Add tofu cubes and stir-fry until golden brown.
4. Add minced garlic and grated ginger, stir-frying for an additional minute.
5. Add broccoli florets and the soy sauce mixture. Stir-fry until broccoli is tender-crisp.
6. Serve the stir-fried tofu and broccoli over cooked brown rice.
7. Enjoy this plant-based Stir-Fried Tofu with Broccoli and Brown Rice for a flavorful dinner!

Nutritional Information: (Per Serving)
➢ Calories: 300
➢ Protein: 15g
➢ Carbohydrates: 40g
➢ Fat: 10g

Roasted Sweet Potato and Black Bean Enchiladas

Indulge in a delicious and hearty dinner with Roasted Sweet Potato and Black Bean Enchiladas. The combination of roasted sweet potatoes, black beans, and flavorful enchilada sauce creates a satisfying and flavorful dish.

Total Time: 40 minutes
Servings: 4

Ingredients:
• 2 large sweet potatoes, peeled and diced
• 1 can (15 oz) black beans, drained and rinsed
• 1 teaspoon cumin
• 1 teaspoon chili powder
• 8 whole wheat or corn tortillas
• 2 cups enchilada sauce
• 1 cup shredded Mexican cheese blend
• Fresh cilantro for garnish (optional)
• Greek yogurt or sour cream for serving

Directions:
1. Preheat the oven to 400°F (200°C).
2. Toss diced sweet potatoes with cumin and chili powder. Roast until tender.
3. In a bowl, mix roasted sweet potatoes and black beans.
4. Warm tortillas and fill each with the sweet potato and black bean mixture.
5. Roll up the tortillas and place them in a baking dish.
6. Pour enchilada sauce over the rolled tortillas and sprinkle with shredded cheese.
7. Bake for 15-20 minutes or until the cheese is melted and bubbly.
8. Garnish with fresh cilantro if desired.
9. Serve these Roasted Sweet Potato and Black Bean Enchiladas with a dollop of Greek yogurt or sour cream.

Nutritional Information: (Per Serving)
➤ Calories: 350
➤ Protein: 15g
➤ Carbohydrates: 50g
➤ Fat: 12g

Herb-Crusted Baked Salmon

Elevate your dinner with Herb-Crusted Baked Salmon, a dish that combines the richness of salmon with a flavorful herb crust. This easy and elegant recipe is perfect for a healthy and delicious meal.

Total Time: 20 minutes
Servings: 2

Ingredients:
- 2 salmon fillets
- 2 tablespoons Dijon mustard
- 1 tablespoon olive oil
- 1/2 cup breadcrumbs (whole wheat or panko)
- 1 tablespoon fresh parsley, chopped
- 1 teaspoon dried thyme
- Salt and pepper to taste
- Lemon wedges for serving

Directions:
1. Preheat the oven to 400°F (200°C).
2. In a bowl, mix Dijon mustard and olive oil.
3. In another bowl, combine breadcrumbs, chopped fresh parsley, dried thyme, salt, and pepper.
4. Brush the top of each salmon fillet with the Dijon mustard mixture.
5. Press the herb and breadcrumb mixture onto the mustard-coated side of the salmon.
6. Place the fillets on a baking sheet and bake for 12-15 minutes or until the salmon is cooked through.
7. Serve the Herb-Crusted Baked Salmon with lemon wedges for a burst of freshness.

Nutritional Information: (Per Serving)
➢ Calories: 300
➢ Protein: 25g
➢ Carbohydrates: 15g
➢ Fat: 15g

Cauliflower Fried Rice with Shrimp

Enjoy a lighter and lower-carb version of a classic with Cauliflower Fried Rice featuring succulent shrimp. This dish is loaded with colorful vegetables and is a tasty alternative to traditional fried rice.

Total Time: 30 minutes
Servings: 4

Ingredients:
- 1 medium cauliflower, grated or riced
- 1 pound shrimp, peeled and deveined
- 2 tablespoons soy sauce
- 1 tablespoon sesame oil
- 2 tablespoons vegetable oil
- 1 cup frozen peas and carrots, thawed
- 3 green onions, chopped
- 2 cloves garlic, minced

- 2 eggs, beaten
- Salt and pepper to taste

Directions:
1. In a wok or large skillet, heat vegetable oil over medium-high heat.
2. Add shrimp and cook until pink and opaque. Remove shrimp and set aside.
3. In the same pan, add grated cauliflower, soy sauce, and sesame oil. Stir-fry until the cauliflower is tender.
4. Push cauliflower to one side of the pan and add beaten eggs. Scramble the eggs until cooked.
5. Combine cooked shrimp, thawed peas and carrots, chopped green onions, and minced garlic with the cauliflower mixture.
6. Stir-fry until all ingredients are well combined and heated through.
7. Season with salt and pepper to taste.
8. Serve this Cauliflower Fried Rice with Shrimp for a flavorful and low-carb dinner!

Nutritional Information: (Per Serving)
- ➢ Calories: 250
- ➢ Protein: 20g
- ➢ Carbohydrates: 10g
- ➢ Fat: 12g

Chicken and Vegetable Curry with Cauliflower Rice

Immerse yourself in the rich and aromatic flavors of Chicken and Vegetable Curry served over a bed of cauliflower rice. This low-carb and nutrient-packed dinner are perfect for satisfying your curry cravings.

Total Time: 40 minutes
Servings: 4

Ingredients:
- 1 pound boneless, skinless chicken thighs, cut into chunks
- 1 tablespoon curry powder
- 1 teaspoon ground turmeric
- 1 teaspoon ground cumin
- 1 teaspoon paprika
- 1 can (14 oz) coconut milk

- 1 cup broccoli florets
- 1 bell pepper, diced
- 1 carrot, sliced
- 1 zucchini, sliced
- Salt and pepper to taste
- Fresh cilantro for garnish (optional)
- Cauliflower rice for serving

Directions:
1. In a bowl, coat chicken chunks with curry powder, ground turmeric, ground cumin, and paprika.
2. In a skillet, brown the seasoned chicken over medium-high heat.
3. Add coconut milk, broccoli, bell pepper, carrot, and zucchini to the skillet.
4. Simmer until chicken is cooked through and vegetables are tender.
5. Season with salt and pepper to taste.
6. Serve the Chicken and Vegetable Curry over cauliflower rice.
7. Garnish with fresh cilantro if desired.
8. Enjoy this flavorful and low-carb Chicken and Vegetable Curry for dinner!

Nutritional Information: (Per Serving)
- Calories: 300
- Protein: 25g
- Carbohydrates: 10g
- Fat: 18g

Grilled Eggplant and Tomato Stacks

Elevate your dinner with Grilled Eggplant and Tomato Stacks, a visually stunning and delicious dish. The layers of grilled eggplant, ripe tomatoes, and melted mozzarella create a perfect harmony of flavors.

Total Time: 30 minutes
Servings: 2

Ingredients:
- 1 large eggplant, sliced into rounds
- 2 large tomatoes, sliced
- 1/2 cup fresh mozzarella, sliced
- Balsamic glaze
- Fresh basil leaves

- Olive oil
- Salt and pepper to taste

Directions:
1. Preheat the grill or grill pan over medium-high heat.
2. Brush eggplant slices with olive oil and season with salt and pepper.
3. Grill eggplant slices until tender, about 2-3 minutes per side.
4. Assemble stacks by layering grilled eggplant, tomato slices, and mozzarella.
5. Drizzle with balsamic glaze and garnish with fresh basil leaves.
6. Serve these Grilled Eggplant and Tomato Stacks for a light and flavorful dinner!

Nutritional Information: (Per Serving)
- Calories: 200
- Protein: 8g
- Carbohydrates: 15g
- Fat: 12g

Lemon Garlic Shrimp Skewers

Delight your taste buds with Lemon Garlic Shrimp Skewers, a quick and flavorful dinner option. The zesty marinade infuses the shrimp with bright flavors, making each bite a burst of freshness.

Total Time: 20 minutes
Servings: 4

Ingredients:
- 1 pound large shrimp, peeled and deveined
- Zest and juice of 1 lemon
- 3 cloves garlic, minced
- 2 tablespoons olive oil
- Fresh parsley, chopped

- Salt and pepper to taste
- Wooden skewers, soaked in water

Directions:
1. In a bowl, mix lemon zest, lemon juice, minced garlic, olive oil, chopped parsley, salt, and pepper.
2. Thread shrimp on skewers and brush with the lemon garlic marinade.
3. Preheat the grill or grill pan over medium-high heat.
4. Grill shrimp skewers for 2-3 minutes per side or until shrimp are opaque.
5. Serve these Lemon Garlic Shrimp Skewers for a light and zesty dinner!

Nutritional Information: (Per Serving)
- Calories: 150
- Protein: 20g
- Carbohydrates: 2g
- Fat: 7g

Baked Chicken Parmesan with Zucchini Noodles

Enjoy a healthier twist on a classic Italian dish with Baked Chicken Parmesan served over zucchini noodles. This dinner option offers the same comforting flavors but with a lighter and low-carb touch.

Total Time: 45 minutes
Servings: 4

Ingredients:
- 4 boneless, skinless chicken breasts
- 1 cup whole wheat breadcrumbs
- 1/2 cup grated Parmesan cheese
- 1 teaspoon dried oregano
- 1 teaspoon dried basil

- Salt and pepper to taste
- 2 eggs, beaten
- 2 cups marinara sauce
- 4 zucchinis, spiralized into noodles
- Fresh basil for garnish (optional)

Directions:
1. Preheat the oven to 400°F (200°C).
2. In a shallow bowl, mix breadcrumbs, Parmesan cheese, dried oregano, dried basil, salt, and pepper.
3. Dip each chicken breast in beaten eggs, then coat with the breadcrumb mixture.
4. Place breaded chicken on a baking sheet and bake for 25-30 minutes or until golden and cooked through.
5. Heat marinara sauce in a saucepan.
6. Spiralize zucchinis into noodles and sauté in a pan until just tender.
7. Serve baked chicken over zucchini noodles, topped with marinara sauce.
8. Garnish with fresh basil if desired.
9. Enjoy this Baked Chicken Parmesan with Zucchini Noodles for a satisfying and wholesome dinner!

Nutritional Information: (Per Serving)
➢ Calories: 350
➢ Protein: 40g
➢ Carbohydrates: 15g
➢ Fat: 15g

Quinoa-Stuffed Acorn Squash

Embrace the flavors of fall with Quinoa-Stuffed Acorn Squash, a hearty and nutritious dinner option. The combination of quinoa, vegetables, and sweet acorn squash creates a wholesome and satisfying meal.

Total Time: 50 minutes
Servings: 2

Ingredients:
- 1 acorn squash, halved and seeds removed
- 1 cup quinoa, cooked
- 1/2 cup black beans, drained and rinsed

- 1/2 cup corn kernels
- 1/2 cup cherry tomatoes, halved
- 1/4 cup red onion, finely chopped
- 1/4 cup feta cheese, crumbled
- Fresh parsley for garnish (optional)
- Olive oil
- Salt and pepper to taste

Directions:
1. Preheat the oven to 375°F (190°C).
2. Rub acorn squash halves with olive oil and season with salt and pepper.
3. Place squash halves, cut side down, on a baking sheet and roast for 30-35 minutes or until tender.
4. In a bowl, mix cooked quinoa, black beans, corn, cherry tomatoes, red onion, and feta cheese.
5. Stuff each roasted acorn squash half with the quinoa mixture.
6. Bake for an additional 10-15 minutes or until heated through.
7. Garnish with fresh parsley if desired.
8. Serve these Quinoa-Stuffed Acorn Squash halves for a wholesome and flavorful dinner!

Nutritional Information: (Per Serving)
- Calories: 400
- Protein: 15g
- Carbohydrates: 60g
- Fat: 10g

Mushroom and Spinach Stuffed Chicken Breast

Treat yourself to a gourmet-inspired dinner with Mushroom and Spinach Stuffed Chicken Breast. This dish features juicy chicken breasts filled with a savory mixture of mushrooms, spinach, and cheese.

Total Time: 40 minutes
Servings: 2

Ingredients:
- 2 boneless, skinless chicken breasts

- 1 cup mushrooms, finely chopped
- 1 cup fresh spinach, chopped
- 1/2 cup ricotta cheese
- 1/4 cup grated Parmesan cheese
- 2 cloves garlic, minced
- 1 tablespoon olive oil
- 1 teaspoon dried thyme
- Salt and pepper to taste

Directions:
1. Preheat the oven to 375°F (190°C).
2. In a pan, sauté chopped mushrooms and minced garlic in olive oil until softened.
3. Add chopped spinach and sauté until wilted. Remove from heat.
4. In a bowl, mix ricotta cheese, Parmesan cheese, dried thyme, salt, and pepper.
5. Butterfly each chicken breast and fill with the mushroom and spinach mixture.
6. Spread the cheese mixture over the spinach and mushrooms.
7. Secure the chicken breasts with toothpicks if needed.
8. Bake for 25-30 minutes or until the chicken is cooked through.
9. Serve these Mushroom and Spinach Stuffed Chicken Breasts for an elegant and flavorful dinner!

Nutritional Information: (Per Serving)
➢ Calories: 350
➢ Protein: 40g
➢ Carbohydrates: 5g
➢ Fat: 18g

Snacking Smartly

Greek Yogurt with Honey and Walnuts

Indulge in a delightful and protein-packed snack with Greek Yogurt topped with sweet honey and crunchy walnuts. This combination offers a balance of creamy, sweet, and nutty flavors, creating a satisfying treat.

Total Time: 5 minutes
Servings: 1

Ingredients:
- 1 cup Greek yogurt
- 1 tablespoon honey
- 2 tablespoons chopped walnuts

Directions:
1. In a bowl, spoon Greek yogurt.
2. Drizzle honey over the yogurt.
3. Sprinkle chopped walnuts on top.
4. Stir gently to combine.
5. Enjoy this Greek Yogurt with Honey and Walnuts for a quick and nutritious snack!

Nutritional Information: (Per Serving)
- Calories: 250
- Protein: 15g
- Carbohydrates: 20g
- Fat: 12g

Fresh Fruit Salad with Lime Mint Dressing

Introduction: Refresh your palate with a vibrant Fresh Fruit Salad featuring a zesty Lime Mint Dressing. This snack is a burst of colors and flavors, providing a sweet and citrusy delight.

Total Time: 15 minutes
Servings: 2

Ingredients:
- 1 cup strawberries, hulled and sliced
- 1 cup pineapple chunks
- 1 cup blueberries
- Juice of 1 lime
- 1 tablespoon honey
- Fresh mint leaves for garnish (optional)

Directions:
1. In a bowl, combine strawberries, pineapple chunks, and blueberries.
2. In a small bowl, whisk together lime juice and honey to create the dressing.
3. Drizzle the Lime Mint Dressing over the fruit salad.
4. Toss gently to coat the fruits.
5. Garnish with fresh mint leaves if desired.
6. Serve this Fresh Fruit Salad with Lime Mint Dressing for a refreshing and vitamin-packed snack!

Nutritional Information: (Per Serving)
- Calories: 150
- Protein: 2g
- Carbohydrates: 40g
- Fat: 1g

Rice Cakes with Hummus and Cherry Tomatoes

Elevate your snack time with Rice Cakes topped with creamy hummus and juicy cherry tomatoes. This combination provides a satisfying crunch along with a burst of Mediterranean-inspired flavors.

Total Time: 10 minutes
Servings: 2

Ingredients:
- 4 rice cakes
- 1/2 cup hummus
- 1 cup cherry tomatoes, halved
- Fresh parsley for garnish (optional)

Directions:
1. Spread a generous layer of hummus on each rice cake.
2. Top with halved cherry tomatoes.
3. Garnish with fresh parsley if desired.
4. Serve these Rice Cakes with Hummus and Cherry Tomatoes for a light and savory snack!

Nutritional Information: (Per Serving)
- Calories: 180
- Protein: 6g
- Carbohydrates: 30g
- Fat: 5g

Guacamole with Baked Tortilla Chips

Dive into a bowl of fresh and flavorful Guacamole paired with crispy Baked Tortilla Chips. This snack offers the creamy richness of avocados combined with the crunch of homemade tortilla chips.

Total Time: 20 minutes
Servings: 4

Ingredients:
- 3 ripe avocados, mashed
- 1 tomato, diced
- 1/4 cup red onion, finely chopped
- 1/4 cup fresh cilantro, chopped
- Juice of 1 lime
- Salt and pepper to taste
- Baked tortilla chips for dipping

Directions:
1. In a bowl, combine mashed avocados, diced tomato, chopped red onion, cilantro, lime juice, salt, and pepper.
2. Mix until well combined.
3. Serve the Guacamole with Baked Tortilla Chips for a satisfying and nutritious snack!

Nutritional Information: (Per Serving)
➢ Calories: 200
➢ Protein: 3g
➢ Carbohydrates: 15g
➢ Fat: 15g

Cottage Cheese with Pineapple Chunks

Enjoy a simple and protein-packed snack with Cottage Cheese paired with sweet and tangy pineapple chunks. This combination provides a quick and easy option for a light and satisfying treat.

Total Time: 5 minutes
Servings: 1

Ingredients:
- 1 cup cottage cheese
- 1/2 cup pineapple chunks

Directions:
1. In a bowl, spoon cottage cheese.

2. Top with pineapple chunks.
3. Stir gently to combine.
4. Enjoy this Cottage Cheese with Pineapple Chunks for a quick and nutritious snack!

Nutritional Information: (Per Serving)
- ➢ Calories: 180
- ➢ Protein: 20g
- ➢ Carbohydrates: 15g
- ➢ Fat: 5g

Celery Sticks with Almond Butter

Energize your snack time with Celery Sticks paired with creamy Almond Butter. This simple and nutritious snack offers a satisfying crunch along with the wholesome goodness of almond butter.

Total Time: 5 minutes
Servings: 2

Ingredients:
- 4 celery sticks
- 4 tablespoons almond butter

Directions:
1. Wash and cut celery sticks into manageable lengths.
2. Spread almond butter along the concave side of each celery stick.
3. Enjoy these Celery Sticks with Almond Butter for a quick and protein-rich snack!

Nutritional Information: (Per Serving)
- ➢ Calories: 150
- ➢ Protein: 6g
- ➢ Carbohydrates: 8g
- ➢ Fat: 12g

Roasted Chickpeas with Cumin and Paprika

Transform humble chickpeas into a flavorful and crunchy snack with Roasted Chickpeas seasoned with cumin and paprika. This snack is not only delicious but also packed with protein and fiber.

Total Time: 40 minutes
Servings: 4

Ingredients:
- 2 cans (15 oz each) chickpeas, drained and rinsed
- 2 tablespoons olive oil
- 1 teaspoon ground cumin
- 1 teaspoon smoked paprika
- Salt to taste

Directions:
1. Preheat the oven to 400°F (200°C).
2. Pat the chickpeas dry with a paper towel.
3. In a bowl, toss chickpeas with olive oil, ground cumin, smoked paprika, and salt.
4. Spread chickpeas on a baking sheet in a single layer.
5. Roast for 30-35 minutes or until crispy, shaking the pan halfway through.
6. Allow to cool before serving.
7. Enjoy these Roasted Chickpeas with Cumin and Paprika for a savory and satisfying snack!

Nutritional Information: (Per Serving)
- Calories: 180
- Protein: 8g
- Carbohydrates: 25g
- Fat: 6g

Sliced Cucumber with Tzatziki Sauce

Immerse yourself in the refreshing flavors of Sliced Cucumber paired with tangy Tzatziki Sauce. This snack provides a crisp and hydrating option with a burst of Mediterranean-inspired taste.

Total Time: 10 minutes
Servings: 2

Ingredients:
- 1 large cucumber, sliced
- 1/2 cup Tzatziki sauce

Directions:
1. Wash and slice the cucumber into rounds.
2. Arrange cucumber slices on a plate.
3. Serve with a side of Tzatziki sauce for dipping.
4. Enjoy these Sliced Cucumbers with Tzatziki Sauce for a cool and flavorful snack!

Nutritional Information: (Per Serving)
- ➤ Calories: 80
- ➤ Protein: 2g
- ➤ Carbohydrates: 10g
- ➤ Fat: 4g

Mixed Nuts and Seeds Trail Mix

Create a wholesome and crunchy snack with a Mixed Nuts and Seeds Trail Mix. Packed with a variety of nuts and seeds, this snack offers a satisfying blend of flavors and textures.

Total Time: 5 minutes
Servings: 4

Ingredients:

- 1/2 cup almonds
- 1/2 cup walnuts
- 1/4 cup pumpkin seeds
- 1/4 cup sunflower seeds
- 1/4 cup dried cranberries
- 1/4 cup dark chocolate chips

1. Directions:
2. In a bowl, combine almonds, walnuts, pumpkin seeds, sunflower seeds, dried cranberries, and dark chocolate chips.
3. Mix well to ensure an even distribution of ingredients.
4. Portion into small snack-sized bags for convenient and portable enjoyment.
5. Enjoy this Mixed Nuts and Seeds Trail Mix for a nutritious and satisfying snack!

Nutritional Information: (Per Serving)
- Calories: 200
- Protein: 6g
- Carbohydrates: 15g
- Fat: 14g

Low Potassium Salsa with Jicama Sticks

Explore a flavorful and potassium-friendly snack with Low Potassium Salsa served with crisp Jicama Sticks. This snack is not only delicious but also tailored for those following a low potassium diet.

Total Time: 15 minutes
Servings: 2

Ingredients:
- 2 cups diced tomatoes
- 1/2 cup diced red onion
- 1/4 cup chopped cilantro
- 1 jalapeño, seeded and minced
- Juice of 1 lime
- Salt to taste
- Jicama sticks for dipping

Directions:

1. In a bowl, combine diced tomatoes, red onion, chopped cilantro, minced jalapeño, lime juice, and salt.
2. Mix well to incorporate flavors.
3. Chill the salsa in the refrigerator for at least 10 minutes.
4. Serve with Jicama sticks for a refreshing and low potassium snack!
5. Enjoy this Low Potassium Salsa with Jicama Sticks for a flavorful and diet-friendly treat!

Nutritional Information: (Per Serving)
➢ Calories: 40
➢ Protein: 1g
➢ Carbohydrates: 10g
➢ Fat: 0g

Desserts

Berry Parfait with Whipped Cream

Indulge in the sweet and vibrant layers of a Berry Parfait with Whipped Cream. This delightful dessert combines the freshness of mixed berries with the airy texture of whipped cream for a treat that's as pleasing to the eyes as it is to the taste buds.

Total Time: 15 minutes
Servings: 2

Ingredients:
- 1 cup mixed berries (strawberries, blueberries, raspberries)
- 1 cup whipped cream
- 2 tablespoons honey or maple syrup
- Fresh mint leaves for garnish (optional)

Directions:
1. In serving glasses, layer mixed berries with whipped cream.
2. Drizzle honey or maple syrup over each layer.
3. Repeat the layers until the glasses are filled.
4. Garnish with fresh mint leaves if desired.
5. Serve this Berry Parfait with Whipped Cream for a visually appealing and delicious dessert!

Nutritional Information: (Per Serving)
- Calories: 200
- Protein: 2g
- Carbohydrates: 25g
- Fat: 12g

Poached Pears in Red Wine

Elevate your dessert experience with Poached Pears in Red Wine. This sophisticated and aromatic dessert features tender pears infused with the rich flavors of red wine, creating a luxurious finale to any meal.

Total Time: 1 hour
Servings: 4

Ingredients:
- 4 ripe but firm pears, peeled and halved
- 1 bottle red wine
- 1 cup granulated sugar
- 1 cinnamon stick
- 4 cloves
- Vanilla ice cream for serving (optional)

Directions:
1. In a saucepan, combine red wine, granulated sugar, cinnamon stick, and cloves.
2. Bring the mixture to a simmer, stirring until the sugar dissolves.
3. Add the peeled and halved pears to the simmering liquid.
4. Poach the pears for 30-40 minutes or until tender.
5. Remove the pears and let them cool slightly.
6. Serve the Poached Pears in Red Wine with a drizzle of the reduced poaching liquid.
7. Optional: Serve with a scoop of vanilla ice cream for an extra indulgence.
8. Enjoy this elegant and flavorful Poached Pears in Red Wine dessert!

Nutritional Information: (Per Serving)
- Calories: 250
- Protein: 1g
- Carbohydrates: 50g
- Fat: 0g

Dark Chocolate Avocado Mousse

Satisfy your chocolate cravings with a healthier twist—Dark Chocolate Avocado Mousse. This creamy and decadent dessert is made with ripe avocados and dark chocolate, creating a guilt-free indulgence.

Total Time: 20 minutes
Servings: 4

Ingredients:
- 2 ripe avocados, peeled and pitted
- 1/2 cup dark chocolate chips, melted
- 1/4 cup cocoa powder
- 1/4 cup maple syrup or agave nectar
- 1 teaspoon vanilla extract
- Pinch of salt
- Fresh berries for garnish (optional)

Directions:
1. In a food processor, blend avocados until smooth.
2. Add melted dark chocolate, cocoa powder, maple syrup, vanilla extract, and a pinch of salt.
3. Blend until all ingredients are well combined and the mixture is creamy.
4. Spoon the Dark Chocolate Avocado Mousse into serving glasses.
5. Chill in the refrigerator for at least 1 hour.
6. Garnish with fresh berries before serving if desired.
7. Enjoy this rich and velvety Dark Chocolate Avocado Mousse for a guilt-free dessert!

Nutritional Information: (Per Serving)
- Calories: 200
- Protein: 3g
- Carbohydrates: 20g
- Fat: 15g

Baked Apple with Cinnamon and Walnuts

Embrace the comforting aroma of a Baked Apple with Cinnamon and Walnuts. This warm and wholesome dessert features tender baked apples infused with cinnamon and topped with crunchy walnuts, creating a simple yet delightful treat.

Total Time: 30 minutes
Servings: 2

Ingredients:
- 2 apples, cored
- 2 tablespoons chopped walnuts
- 1 tablespoon honey or maple syrup
- 1 teaspoon ground cinnamon
- Greek yogurt for serving (optional)

Directions:
1. Preheat the oven to 375°F (190°C).
2. Place cored apples in a baking dish.
3. In a small bowl, mix chopped walnuts, honey or maple syrup, and ground cinnamon.
4. Stuff each apple with the walnut mixture.
5. Bake for 20-25 minutes or until the apples are tender.
6. Serve the Baked Apples with Cinnamon and Walnuts.
7. Optional: Serve with a dollop of Greek yogurt for added creaminess.
8. Enjoy this cozy and nutritious dessert!

Nutritional Information: (Per Serving)
- Calories: 180
- Protein: 2g
- Carbohydrates: 40g
- Fat: 5g

Coconut Milk Rice Pudding

Transport your taste buds to a tropical paradise with Coconut Milk Rice Pudding. This creamy and aromatic dessert is infused with coconut milk, creating a luscious and satisfying sweet treat.

Total Time: 1 hour
Servings: 4

Ingredients:
- 1 cup Arborio rice
- 1 can (14 oz) coconut milk
- 2 cups almond milk
- 1/2 cup granulated sugar
- 1 teaspoon vanilla extract
- Pinch of salt
- Toasted coconut flakes for garnish (optional)

Directions:
1. In a saucepan, combine Arborio rice, coconut milk, almond milk, granulated sugar, vanilla extract, and a pinch of salt.
2. Bring the mixture to a simmer, stirring occasionally.
3. Simmer on low heat for 40-45 minutes or until the rice is cooked and the pudding has thickened.
4. Remove from heat and let it cool slightly.
5. Spoon the Coconut Milk Rice Pudding into serving bowls.
6. Optional: Garnish with toasted coconut flakes for extra flavor and texture.
7. Enjoy this indulgent and tropical Coconut Milk Rice Pudding for a delightful dessert!

Nutritional Information: (Per Serving)
- Calories: 300
- Protein: 5g
- Carbohydrates: 50g
- Fat: 10g

Mango Sorbet with Mint

Cool down with the refreshing taste of Mango Sorbet with Mint. This tropical dessert combines the sweetness of ripe mangoes with the invigorating essence of fresh mint, creating a delightful and palate-cleansing treat.

Total Time: 4 hours (including freezing time)
Servings: 4

Ingredients:
- 2 large ripe mangoes, peeled and diced
- 1/4 cup fresh mint leaves
- 1/4 cup honey or agave nectar
- Juice of 1 lime
- Mint leaves for garnish (optional)

Directions:
1. In a blender, combine diced mangoes, fresh mint leaves, honey or agave nectar, and lime juice.
2. Blend until smooth and well combined.
3. Pour the mixture into a shallow dish and freeze for at least 4 hours or until firm.
4. Before serving, let the sorbet sit at room temperature for a few minutes to soften.
5. Scoop into serving bowls, garnish with mint leaves if desired.
6. Enjoy this Mango Sorbet with Mint for a tropical and cooling dessert!

Nutritional Information: (Per Serving)
- Calories: 120
- Protein: 1g
- Carbohydrates: 30g
- Fat: 0.5g

Low Potassium Fruit Sorbet

Dive into a delightful and kidney-friendly dessert with Low Potassium Fruit Sorbet. This sorbet features a medley of low potassium fruits, ensuring a delicious and suitable treat for those following a restricted potassium diet.

Total Time: 4 hours (including freezing time)
Servings: 4

Ingredients:
- 1 cup strawberries, hulled
- 1 cup blueberries
- 1 cup pineapple chunks
- 1/4 cup honey or maple syrup
- Juice of 1 lemon
- Fresh mint leaves for garnish (optional)

Directions:
1. In a blender, combine strawberries, blueberries, pineapple chunks, honey or maple syrup, and lemon juice.
2. Blend until smooth and well combined.
3. Pour the mixture into a shallow dish and freeze for at least 4 hours or until firm.
4. Before serving, let the sorbet sit at room temperature for a few minutes to soften.
5. Scoop into serving bowls, garnish with fresh mint leaves if desired.
6. Enjoy this Low Potassium Fruit Sorbet for a kidney-friendly and flavorful dessert!

Nutritional Information: (Per Serving)
- Calories: 100
- Protein: 1g
- Carbohydrates: 25g
- Fat: 0.5g

Angel Food Cake with Berries

Delight in the light and airy goodness of Angel Food Cake with Berries. This classic dessert combines a sponge-like cake with a medley of fresh berries, creating a sweet and satisfying treat.

Total Time: 1 hour
Servings: 8

Ingredients:
- 1 store-bought or homemade angel food cake
- 1 cup strawberries, hulled and sliced
- 1 cup blueberries
- 1 cup raspberries
- 1 cup blackberries
- Whipped cream for serving (optional)
- Mint leaves for garnish (optional)

Directions:
1. Slice the angel food cake into individual servings.
2. Arrange cake slices on serving plates.
3. Top with a generous amount of sliced strawberries, blueberries, raspberries, and blackberries.
4. Optional: Serve with a dollop of whipped cream and garnish with mint leaves.
5. Enjoy this Angel Food Cake with Berries for a light and fruity dessert!

Nutritional Information: (Per Serving)
- Calories: 150
- Protein: 3g
- Carbohydrates: 35g
- Fat: 0g

Almond Flour Chocolate Chip Cookies

Indulge in a gluten-free and lower potassium dessert with Almond Flour Chocolate Chip Cookies. These cookies are made with almond flour, providing a delicious alternative for those with dietary restrictions.

Total Time: 30 minutes
Servings: 12

Ingredients:
- 2 cups almond flour
- 1/2 cup coconut oil, melted
- 1/2 cup maple syrup or agave nectar
- 1 teaspoon vanilla extract
- 1/2 teaspoon baking soda
- 1/4 teaspoon salt
- 1/2 cup dark chocolate chips

Directions:
1. Preheat the oven to 350°F (180°C) and line a baking sheet with parchment paper.
2. In a bowl, combine almond flour, melted coconut oil, maple syrup or agave nectar, vanilla extract, baking soda, and salt.
3. Mix until a dough forms.
4. Fold in dark chocolate chips.
5. Scoop tablespoons of dough and place them on the prepared baking sheet.
6. Flatten each cookie with the back of a fork.
7. Bake for 12-15 minutes or until the edges are golden.
8. Allow the cookies to cool on the baking sheet for a few minutes before transferring to a wire rack.
9. Enjoy these Almond Flour Chocolate Chip Cookies for a gluten-free and kidney-friendly dessert!

Nutritional Information: (Per Serving)
- Calories: 180
- Protein: 4g
- Carbohydrates: 15g
- Fat: 12g

Pomegranate and Orange Salad

Refresh your palate with the vibrant and juicy flavors of Pomegranate and Orange Salad. This dessert is a simple yet elegant combination of sweet citrus and tart pomegranate seeds, creating a refreshing and nutrient-rich treat.

Total Time: 15 minutes
Servings: 4

Ingredients:
- 2 oranges, peeled and segmented
- 1 cup pomegranate seeds
- 1 tablespoon honey
- Fresh mint leaves for garnish (optional)

Directions:
1. In a bowl, combine orange segments and pomegranate seeds.
2. Drizzle honey over the fruit and gently toss to coat.
3. Chill in the refrigerator for 10 minutes.
4. Serve the Pomegranate and Orange Salad in individual bowls.
5. Optional: Garnish with fresh mint leaves for added freshness.
6. Enjoy this light and vitamin-packed dessert!

Nutritional Information: (Per Serving)
- Calories: 80
- Protein: 1g
- Carbohydrates: 20g
- Fat: 0.5g

Smoothies

Spinach and Pineapple Smoothie

Energize your day with the vibrant and nutrient-packed Spinach and Pineapple Smoothie. This green delight combines the goodness of leafy spinach with the tropical sweetness of pineapple, creating a refreshing and health-conscious beverage.

Total Time: 5 minutes
Servings: 2

Ingredients:
- 2 cups fresh spinach leaves
- 1 cup pineapple chunks
- 1 banana, peeled
- 1/2 cup Greek yogurt
- 1 cup coconut water
- Ice cubes (optional)

Directions:
1. In a blender, combine fresh spinach leaves, pineapple chunks, banana, Greek yogurt, and coconut water.
2. Blend until smooth and creamy.
3. Add ice cubes if a colder consistency is desired and blend again.
4. Pour into glasses and enjoy this Spinach and Pineapple Smoothie for a nutrient-packed start to your day!

Nutritional Information: (Per Serving)
- Calories: 150
- Protein: 5g
- Carbohydrates: 30g
- Fat: 2g

Berry Blast Smoothie with Almond Milk

Kickstart your morning with the refreshing and antioxidant-rich Berry Blast Smoothie with Almond Milk. This vibrant concoction combines a medley of berries with the creamy goodness of almond milk for a delightful and wholesome sip.

Total Time: 5 minutes
Servings: 2

Ingredients:
- 1 cup mixed berries (strawberries, blueberries, raspberries)
- 1 banana, peeled
- 1/2 cup almond milk
- 1/2 cup Greek yogurt
- 1 tablespoon honey or agave nectar
- Ice cubes (optional)

Directions:
1. In a blender, combine mixed berries, banana, almond milk, Greek yogurt, and honey or agave nectar.
2. Blend until smooth and well combined.
3. Add ice cubes if a colder consistency is desired and blend again.
4. Pour into glasses and savor the refreshing Berry Blast Smoothie with Almond Milk!

Nutritional Information: (Per Serving)
- Calories: 120
- Protein: 4g
- Carbohydrates: 25g
- Fat: 2.5g

Kiwi and Banana Smoothie

Transport your taste buds to a tropical paradise with the Kiwi and Banana Smoothie. This green and fruity blend combines the unique flavor of kiwi with the creaminess of banana, offering a delightful and vitamin-packed beverage.

Total Time: 5 minutes
Servings: 2

Ingredients:
- 2 kiwis, peeled and sliced
- 1 banana, peeled
- 1/2 cup plain yogurt
- 1/2 cup orange juice
- 1 tablespoon chia seeds
- Ice cubes (optional)

Directions:
1. In a blender, combine sliced kiwis, banana, plain yogurt, orange juice, and chia seeds.
2. Blend until smooth and creamy.
3. Add ice cubes if a colder consistency is desired and blend again.
4. Pour into glasses and enjoy the tropical goodness of the Kiwi and Banana Smoothie!

Nutritional Information: (Per Serving)
- Calories: 160
- Protein: 4g
- Carbohydrates: 30g
- Fat: 3g

Green Apple and Kale Smoothie

Embrace the power of greens with the Green Apple and Kale Smoothie. This vibrant concoction combines the crispness of green apple with the nutritional powerhouse of kale, creating a refreshing and health-conscious beverage.

Total Time: 5 minutes
Servings: 2

Ingredients:
- 1 green apple, cored and sliced
- 1 cup kale leaves, stems removed
- 1/2 cucumber, peeled and sliced
- 1/2 lemon, juiced
- 1 tablespoon fresh ginger, grated
- 1 cup coconut water
- Ice cubes (optional)

Directions:
1. In a blender, combine green apple slices, kale leaves, cucumber slices, lemon juice, grated fresh ginger, and coconut water.
2. Blend until smooth and well combined.
3. Add ice cubes if a colder consistency is desired and blend again.
4. Pour into glasses and enjoy the crisp and invigorating Green Apple and Kale Smoothie!

Nutritional Information: (Per Serving)
- Calories: 100
- Protein: 3g
- Carbohydrates: 25g
- Fat: 1g

Mango Coconut Smoothie

Transport yourself to a tropical paradise with the luscious and creamy Mango Coconut Smoothie. This exotic blend combines the sweetness of ripe mangoes with the rich and velvety texture of coconut milk, creating a smooth and indulgent sip.

Total Time: 5 minutes
Servings: 2

Ingredients:
- 1 cup ripe mango chunks
- 1/2 cup coconut milk
- 1/2 cup Greek yogurt
- 1 tablespoon honey or agave nectar
- 1/2 teaspoon vanilla extract
- Ice cubes (optional)

Directions:
1. In a blender, combine ripe mango chunks, coconut milk, Greek yogurt, honey or agave nectar, and vanilla extract.
2. Blend until smooth and creamy.
3. Add ice cubes if a colder consistency is desired and blend again.
4. Pour into glasses and savor the tropical bliss of the Mango Coconut Smoothie!

Nutritional Information: (Per Serving)
- Calories: 180
- Protein: 5g
- Carbohydrates: 30g
- Fat: 5g

Blueberry Almond Butter Smoothie

Start your day on a nutritious note with the Blueberry Almond Butter Smoothie. Packed with antioxidants from blueberries and a protein boost from almond butter, this smoothie is a delicious and energizing choice for breakfast or a snack.

Total Time: 5 minutes
Servings: 2

Ingredients:
- 1 cup blueberries (fresh or frozen)
- 2 tablespoons almond butter
- 1 banana, peeled
- 1 cup almond milk
- 1 tablespoon honey or maple syrup
- Ice cubes (optional)

Directions:
1. In a blender, combine blueberries, almond butter, banana, almond milk, and honey or maple syrup.
2. Blend until smooth and creamy.
3. Add ice cubes if a colder consistency is desired and blend again.
4. Pour into glasses and enjoy the antioxidant-rich goodness of the Blueberry Almond Butter Smoothie!

Nutritional Information: (Per Serving)
- ➢ Calories: 200
- ➢ Protein: 5g
- ➢ Carbohydrates: 30g
- ➢ Fat: 8g

Avocado and Spinach Detox Smoothie

Cleanse and rejuvenate with the Avocado and Spinach Detox Smoothie. This green powerhouse combines nutrient-dense avocado with detoxifying spinach, creating a smoothie that not only tastes refreshing but also contributes to your overall well-being.

Total Time: 5 minutes
Servings: 2

Ingredients:
- 1 ripe avocado, peeled and pitted
- 2 cups fresh spinach leaves
- 1 green apple, cored and sliced
- 1/2 cucumber, peeled and sliced
- 1/2 lemon, juiced
- 1 cup coconut water
- Ice cubes (optional)

Directions:
1. In a blender, combine ripe avocado, fresh spinach leaves, green apple slices, cucumber slices, lemon juice, and coconut water.
2. Blend until smooth and well combined.
3. Add ice cubes if a colder consistency is desired and blend again.
4. Pour into glasses and enjoy the detoxifying benefits of the Avocado and Spinach Detox Smoothie!

Nutritional Information: (Per Serving)
- Calories: 180
- Protein: 3g
- Carbohydrates: 25g
- Fat: 10g

Peach and Ginger Smoothie

Awaken your taste buds with the zesty Peach and Ginger Smoothie. The combination of sweet peaches and the warmth of ginger creates a flavorful and invigorating drink that's perfect for a morning pick-me-up.

Total Time: 5 minutes
Servings: 2

Ingredients:
- 2 cups sliced peaches (fresh or frozen)
- 1 tablespoon fresh ginger, grated
- 1 banana, peeled
- 1/2 cup Greek yogurt
- 1 cup coconut water
- 1 tablespoon honey or agave nectar
- Ice cubes (optional)

Directions:
1. In a blender, combine sliced peaches, grated fresh ginger, banana, Greek yogurt, coconut water, and honey or agave nectar.
2. Blend until smooth and well combined.
3. Add ice cubes if a colder consistency is desired and blend again.
4. Pour into glasses and savor the delightful combination of Peach and Ginger in this refreshing smoothie!

Nutritional Information: (Per Serving)
- Calories: 160
- Protein: 4g
- Carbohydrates: 30g
- Fat: 2g

Pineapple Mint Smoothie

Cool down with the tropical vibes of the Pineapple Mint Smoothie. This refreshing blend of sweet pineapple and invigorating mint is the perfect way to quench your thirst and uplift your senses.

Total Time: 5 minutes
Servings: 2

Ingredients:
- 1 cup pineapple chunks
- 1/2 cup fresh mint leaves
- 1 banana, peeled
- 1/2 cup coconut water
- 1/2 cup Greek yogurt
- 1 tablespoon honey or agave nectar
- Ice cubes (optional)

Directions:
1. In a blender, combine pineapple chunks, fresh mint leaves, banana, coconut water, Greek yogurt, and honey or agave nectar.
2. Blend until smooth and well combined.
3. Add ice cubes if a colder consistency is desired and blend again.
4. Pour into glasses and enjoy the tropical paradise of the Pineapple Mint Smoothie!

Nutritional Information: (Per Serving)
- Calories: 140
- Protein: 3g
- Carbohydrates: 30g
- Fat: 1.5g

Cucumber and Mint Smoothie

Rehydrate and rejuvenate with the Cucumber and Mint Smoothie. This hydrating blend combines crisp cucumber with refreshing mint, creating a light and invigorating smoothie that's perfect for hot days or post-workout replenishment.

Total Time: 5 minutes
Servings: 2

Ingredients:
- 1 cucumber, peeled and sliced
- 1/2 cup fresh mint leaves
- 1 green apple, cored and sliced
- 1/2 lemon, juiced
- 1 cup coconut water
- 1 tablespoon honey or agave nectar
- Ice cubes (optional)

Directions:
1. In a blender, combine sliced cucumber, fresh mint leaves, green apple slices, lemon juice, coconut water, and honey or agave nectar.
2. Blend until smooth and well combined.
3. Add ice cubes if a colder consistency is desired and blend again.
4. Pour into glasses and enjoy the hydrating goodness of the Cucumber and Mint Smoothie!

Nutritional Information: (Per Serving)
- Calories: 120
- Protein: 2g
- Carbohydrates: 25g
- Fat: 0.5g

Conclusion

As we arrive at the conclusion of this insightful journey through the "Low Potassium Diet Cookbook for Seniors," it's time to reflect on the valuable lessons learned and look ahead to a future marked by improved health and well-being. This concluding chapter serves as a compass, guiding readers through a recap of key takeaways and offering a roadmap for maintaining a long-term low potassium lifestyle.

In this concluding section, we revisit the fundamental principles and key takeaways that have been woven throughout the book. From understanding the importance of a low potassium diet to mastering the art of identifying high potassium foods, readers are reminded of the building blocks that form the foundation of a kidney-friendly lifestyle.

The success stories shared earlier in the book, exemplified by individuals like Mary, serve as beacons of inspiration. These stories underscore the real-world impact of embracing a low potassium diet, showcasing not only the physical improvements but also the enhanced quality of life and well-being that can result from dietary modifications.

Crucial insights from each chapter are synthesized, creating a comprehensive overview that reinforces the reader's understanding of the intricacies of a low potassium diet. Whether it's learning to stock a low potassium pantry, creating nutrient-rich meal plans, or navigating social situations, the key takeaways provide a holistic understanding that empowers individuals to make informed choices in their daily lives.

As we bid farewell to the structured chapters of this cookbook, the concluding section shifts the focus towards the future. It addresses the importance of continuity and long-term commitment to a low potassium lifestyle. Readers are encouraged to view this journey not as a short-term intervention but as a sustainable and enduring way of life.

This book explores strategies for maintaining motivation and discipline, acknowledging that lifestyle changes require ongoing dedication. It provides tips on integrating the newfound knowledge and skills into daily routines, ensuring that the principles of a low potassium diet become second nature over time.

Emphasizing the role of ongoing support, the conclusion encourages readers to stay connected with healthcare professionals, support groups, and loved ones. Building a network of encouragement and understanding can significantly contribute to the sustained success of a low potassium lifestyle.

In closing, the conclusion serves as a call to action—a reminder that the journey does not end with the last page of this cookbook. Instead, it marks the beginning of a new chapter in which the reader is the author of their own health story. By embracing the principles outlined in this comprehensive guide and maintaining a commitment to long-term well-being, readers are poised to continue thriving on their low potassium journey, savoring a life enriched by health, vitality, and the joy of mindful living.

Manufactured by Amazon.ca
Acheson, AB

11712460R00048